VICTORIA AND ALBERT MUSEUM

Early Keyboard Instruments

by

RAYMOND RUSSELL

F.S.A.

LONDON
HER MAJESTY'S STATIONERY OFFICE
1959

EARLY KEYBOARD INSTRUMENTS

THE early domestic keyboard instruments belong to two basic families: that in which the strings are plucked, and that in which they are struck. To the first family belong the *harpsichord*, in shape like a narrow grand pianoforte, the *spinet*, smaller and either polygonal (plate 8) or wing shaped (plate 23), and the *virginal*, which is the oblong counterpart of the spinet. All these derive from attempts to mechanize the mediaeval psaltery, an instrument in which the strings are plucked by the fingers or by a plectrum held by the player.

The second family has only one member: the *clavichord*. The strings of the clavichord are made to sound by wedge shaped pieces of brass (*tangents*) about $\frac{1}{2}$ inch high, which stand on each key beneath the appropriate strings. When the keys are depressed the tangents rise up and strike the strings; they also determine the vibrating length of each string, for the clavichord has only one bridge. It is in fact a set of *monochords* controlled by a keyboard.

These were the keyboard instruments in common use from the fifteenth to the early years of the nineteenth century. They first developed in Italy, and the majority of sixteenth century survivors of all kinds are Italian. But in the latter half of that century a school of harpsichord and virginal making developed in Antwerp, then a great port and centre of European commerce; and the Flemish instruments, produced in the hundred years before about 1675, filled the greater part of world demand. From the middle of the seventeenth century, the influence of the Antwerp workshops encouraged the development of national schools of instrument making in other countries. France produced spinets and harpsichords, and also specialised in rebuilding and modernising the old Flemish instruments, which were always valued for their good tone. Germany built harpsichords, but was more particularly noted for clavichords, developing and perfecting the large classical models with a five octave compass, for which C. P. E. Bach and others composed a fine repertoire in the mid and late eighteenth century. England had built virginals on the Flemish model in the seventeenth century, but by about 1675 the wing shaped spinet had taken their place, and this remained popular as the equivalent of our upright pianoforte, for the next hundred years or more. London was also the birthplace of a very large number of good harpsichords, built between 1700 and 1800.

The Museum is rich in sixteenth century Italian instruments of fine quality, and these include the oldest surviving instrument known today: a harpsichord of 1521. There is a remarkable virginal, and also three harpsichords, from the Low Countries, the latter coming from the workshop of the famous Ruckers family in Antwerp. France is represented by the beautiful lacquered harpsichord by Pascal Taskin of Paris, the instrument maker to Louis XV and XVI. The German clavichord by Fritz of Brunswick is a splendid example of the real classical clavichord, for which so many eighteenth century German masters composed. The earliest surviving— and the only sixteenth century—English harpsichord is the *harpsichord organ* built by a Fleming, Theeuwes, when at work in London in 1579. From the seventeenth century there are two oblong English virginals and an example of the spinet which replaced them. There are four eighteenth century London spinets and three harpsichords; the harpsichord by Shudi and Broadwood, 1782, was the largest model made in London. The collection of twenty eight instruments is well constructed to demonstrate the general history of the different instruments which preceded the pianoforte.

Pianofortes began to appear in numbers in the 1760s, and the early compact shape, low cost, tone, and ability to play loud or soft at the command of touch alone, a factor in which its predecessors were in varying degree deficient, won the day for hammer action by about 1780. Late eighteenth century harpsichords were consequently built with expressive devices, unknown in the classical period of J. S. Bach and François Couperin fifty years before, which were attempts to rescue the instrument from its rapidly declining popularity. Such devices as the *Machine* stop, for changing the stops by means of a pedal, and the *Venetian swell*, appear in the two late harpsichords by Kirckman and Shudi.

This picture book does not show all the instruments in the Museum: a small Italian spinet, three English spinets (by Thomas Hitchcock, Mahoon, and Baker Harris), an English clavichord, and a small German virginal, are not illustrated. The author has selected the plates to show instruments 1. which are the earliest, of the best musical quality, the most typical as regards decoration, and associated with the best makers; 2. according to their development and national schools; 3. according to their basic musical design: harpsichords of both Italian and Flemish origin, spinets both polygonal and wing shaped, the virginal, and the clavichord.

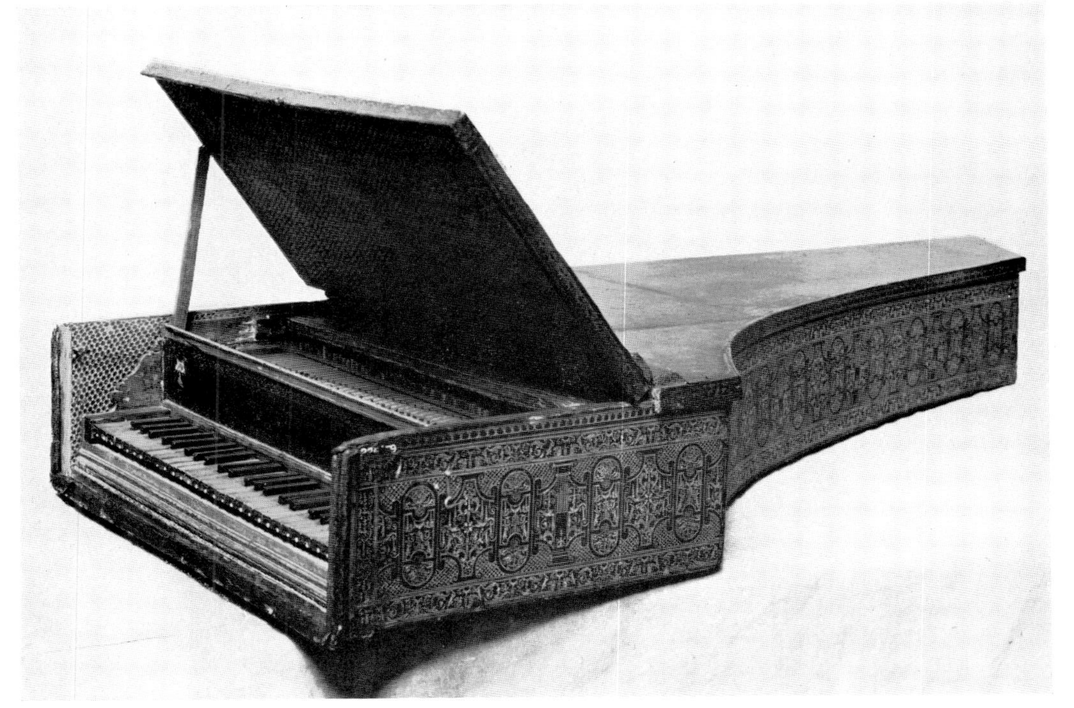

1. Harpsichord made in Rome by Jerome of Bologna, 1521.   This is the oldest known harpsichord.
(226–1879)

2. Spinet by Giovanni Francesco Antegnati of Brescia, 1537.   The spinet can be taken out of the painted case.

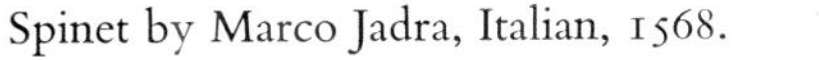

3. Spinet by Annibale dei Rossi of Milan, 1555.　(156–1869)

4. Spinet by Marco Jadra, Italian, 1568.　(155–1869)

5. Harpsichord by Giovanni Antonio Baffo of Venice, 1574.   This harpsichord, by the most distinguished Italian maker, can be removed from the outer painted case.   (6007–1859)

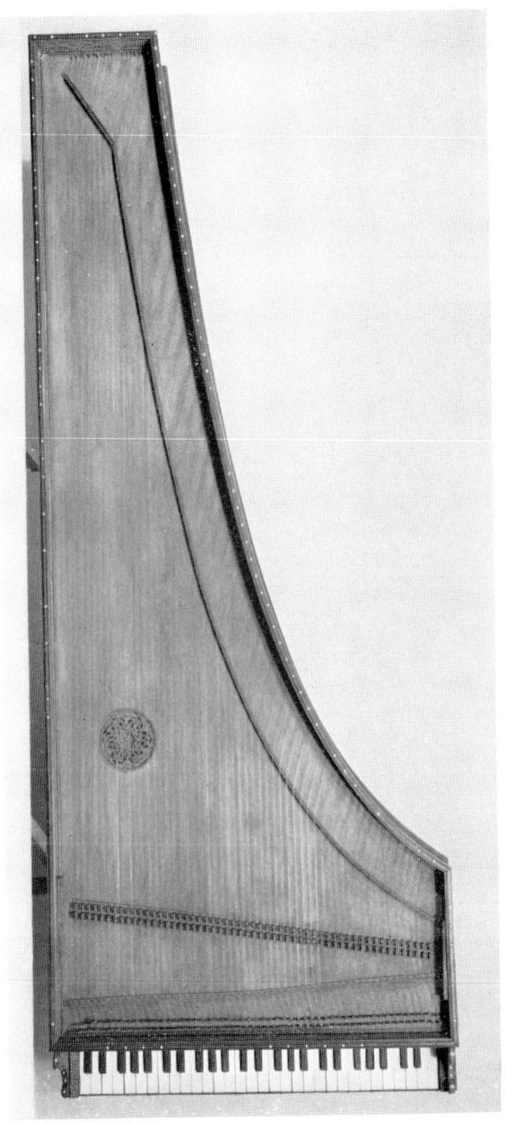

6. Soundboard of the preceding harpsichord.   The jack rail has been removed to show the two rows of jacks.   (6007–1859)

7. Spinet by Annibale dei Rossi of Milan, 1577. The case is inlaid with 1928 precious and semi precious stones.
(809–1869)

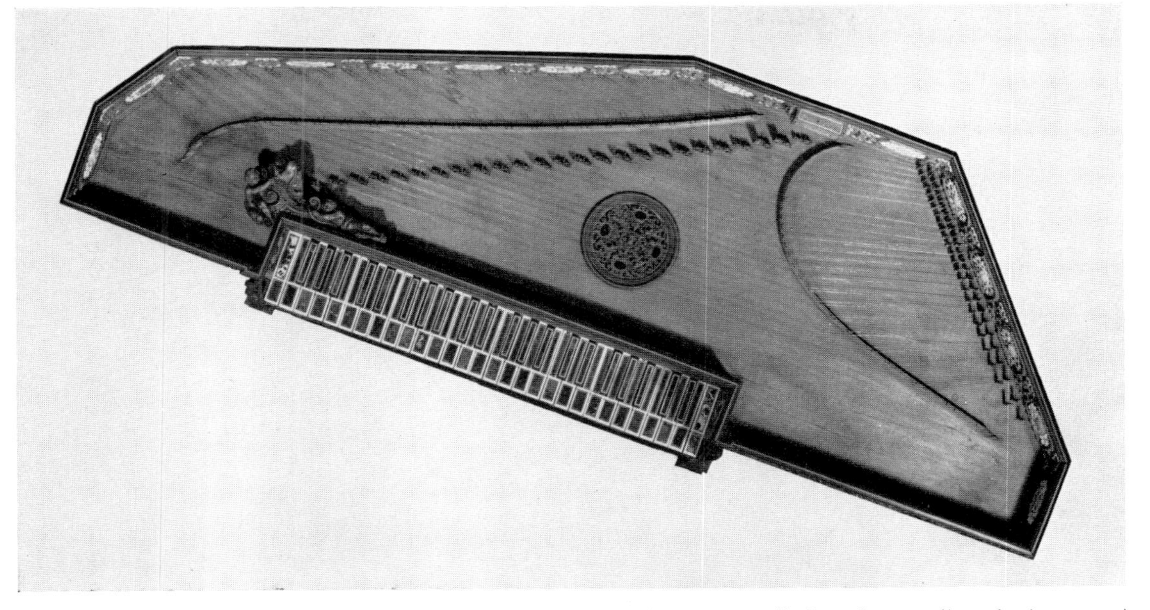

8. Soundboard of the preceding spinet. Observe the finely carved *rose* or soundhole in the soundboard. (809–1869)

9. Hexagonal Italian spinet, 16th century. The spinet has been removed from its outer case. Observe the arms of Queen Elizabeth I, to whom the spinet probably belonged, to the left of the keyboard.   (19–1887)

10. Virginal, Italian, 16th century. The decoration is in coloured glass, silver, and enamel on copper. (402–1872)

11. Virginal, Flemish, 1568. This virginal, built at quint pitch, was made for William, Duke of Cleves, Berg, and Jülich (1516–92). (447–1896)

12. Harpsichord by Jan Ruckers of Antwerp, 1634. This harpsichord, at Ham House, preserves much of its original decoration. The stand is of later date.

(HH–109)

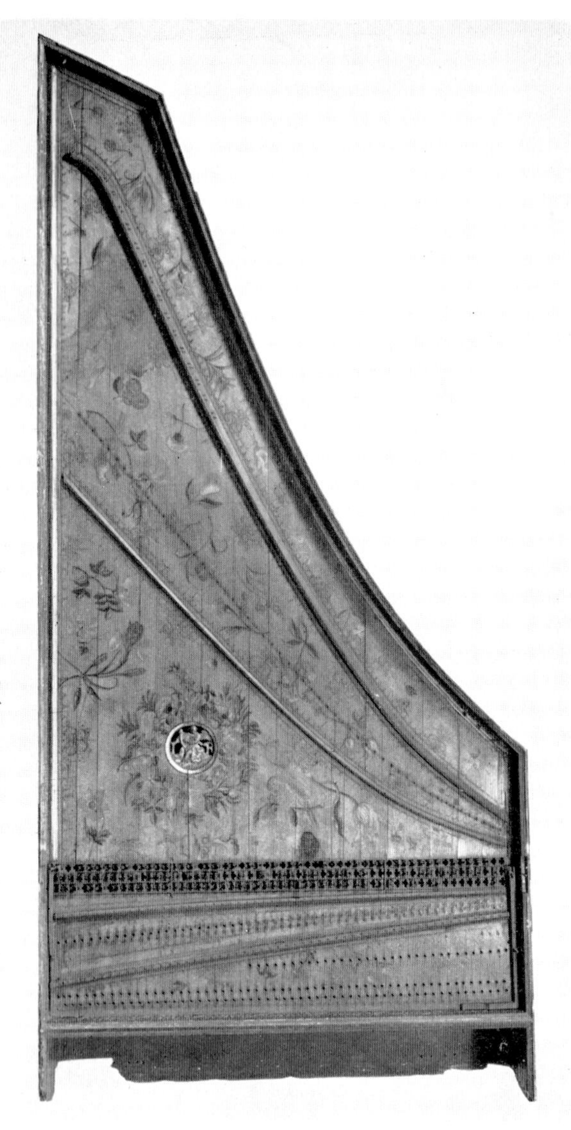

13. Harpsichord, by Jan Ruckers of Antwerp, 1639. This harpsichord, the keys of which are missing, was the property of Queen Charlotte, Consort of King George III. (1739–1869)

14. Harpsichord by Andries Ruckers (the younger) of Antwerp, 1651. The two keyboards are mid eighteenth century English work.   (1079–1868)

15. Harpsichord by Pascal Taskin of Paris, 1786. The narrow keyboard of this harpsichord, too small for the adult hand, suggests that it was made for a child. (1121–1869)

16. Harpsichord and Organ combined, by Lodewijk Theeuwes of London, 1579. This is the oldest known English harpsichord. (125–1890)

17. Virginal by Thomas White of London, 1642. The case is decorated with gilt and embossed paper. (W.11–1933)

18. Soundboard of the preceding virginal. The jack rail has been removed to show the position of the jacks. (W.11–1933)

19. Virginal by John Loosemore of Exeter, 1655. The decoration is typical of the oblong English virginals, all of which are of 17th century date. (813-1873)

20. Spinet by John Player of London, second half of 17th century. The common domestic keyboard instrument which replaced the oblong virginal in England.   (466–1882)

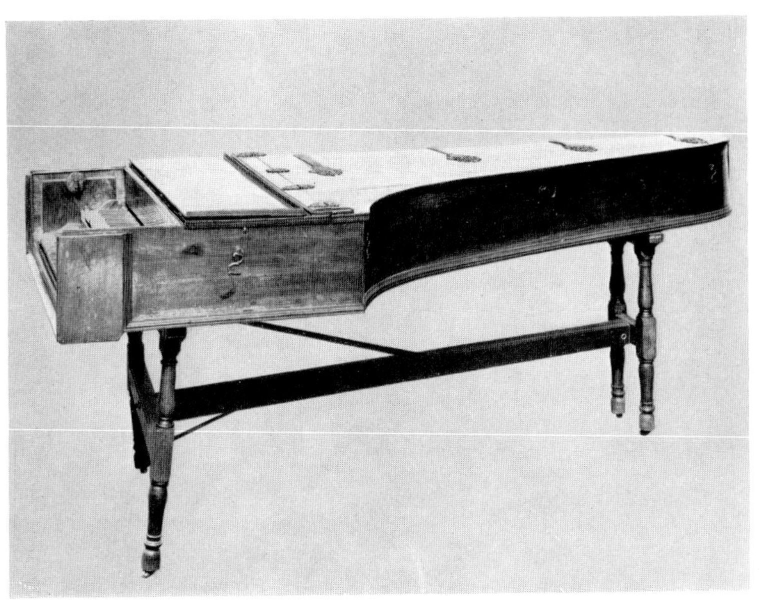

21. Harpsichord by Thomas Hitchcock of London, *circa* 1720. There are two
manuals and three sets of strings: two at eight and one at four foot pitch.

(126–1890)

22. Spinet by John Crang of London, 1758. The small English keyboard instrument of the period 1700–1775, equivalent to the upright pianoforte of today.

(W.16–1947)

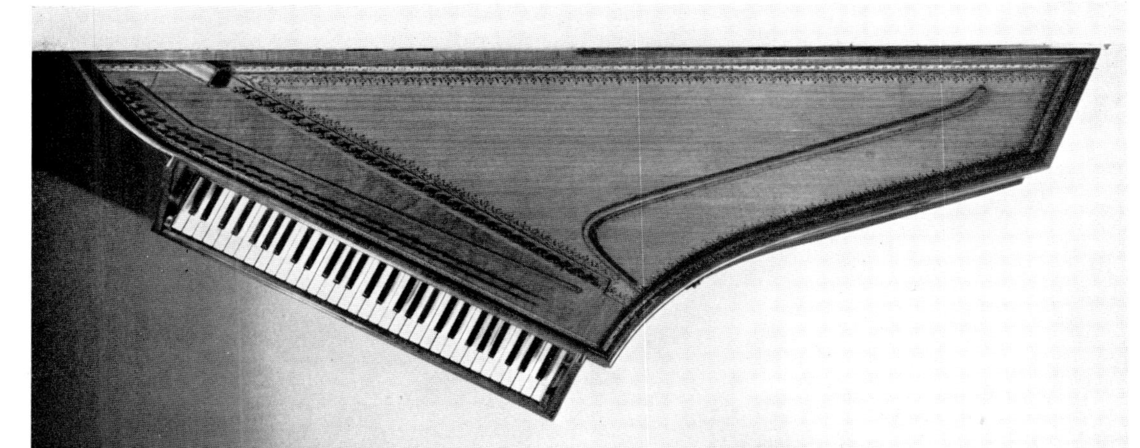

23. Soundboard of the preceding spinet. In design the English spinet is like a harpsichord in which the strings have been brought round to form an angle with the keys.

(W.16–1947)

24. Harpsichord by Jacob and Abraham Kirckman of London, 1776. The equivalent of our grand pianoforte, during the larger part of the eighteenth century. In the Bethnal Green Museum. (W.43–1927)

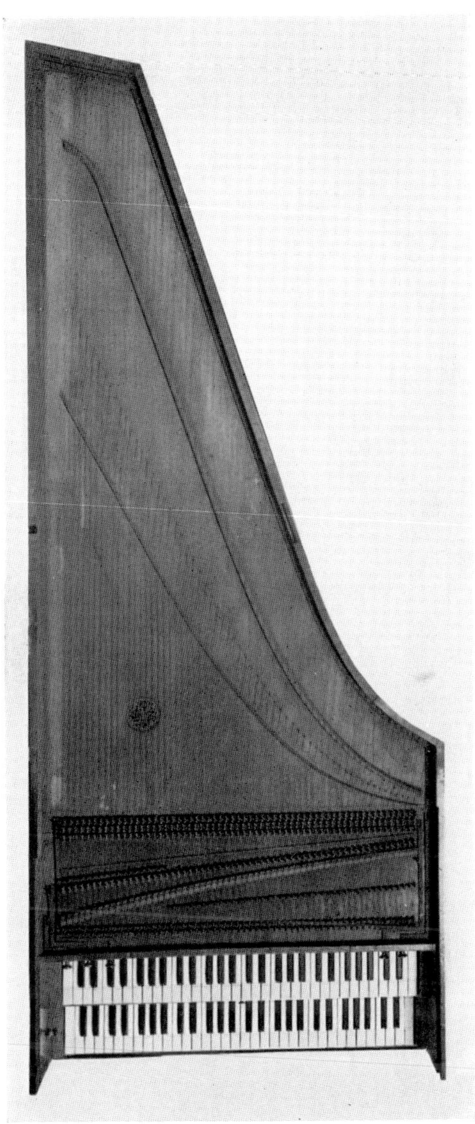

25. Soundboard of the preceding harpsichord. There are six stops: machine, harp, lute, two unisons and one four foot. A typical large model English harpsichord.   (W.43–1927)

26. Harpsichord by Shudi and Broadwood of London, 1782. There are the same stops as in Plate 25. The pedals are (left) Machine, (right) Venetian swell.

(W.13–1943)

27. Clavichord by Barthold Fritz of Brunswick, 1751. A typical large German clavichord, 5 feet 10 inches long, for which many 18th century German masters composed.   (339–1882)

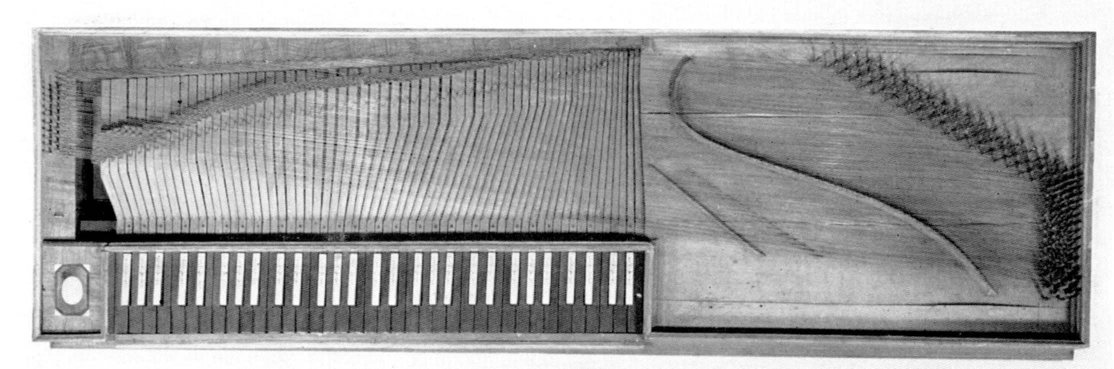

28. Soundboard of the preceding clavichord. Compass: five octaves and a third. There are two eight foot strings for each key, and a four foot string as well for the lowest twenty keys. (339–1882)